A Commentary on the Book of James in the New Testament

Reverend Loyce C. Collins

ISBN 979-8-88832-085-3 (paperback)
ISBN 979-8-89043-520-0 (hardcover)
ISBN 979-8-88832-086-0 (digital)

Christian Faith Publishing
832 Park Avenue
Meadville, PA 16335
www.christianfaithpublishing.com

Contents

Foreword

This commentary book is in the hands of those who love the Word of God. I have known the author for over twenty-eight years. I'm so glad God gave him the inspiration to choose the book of James and the courage to give his thoughts on the book of James. I know his parents as well as mine would have been very proud of him today.

I was one of the first to read this commentary book. I can say it has encouraged my heart. It has helped me learn of my own faith in God while facing any trial in my life. This commentary book has also helped me understand the joy and patience only God gives while going through a trial. I may not understand or believe what is happening at the time, but I must only trust and believe God for the outcome. And this commentary book has helped me understand that it's not only my faith but also my works as I act on God's Word.

I pray this commentary book will help those who read it receive the revelation that God is with them no matter what you face in life.

Thank you, Reverend Loyce Collins, for your own trials that we have faced together. The truth is that we know our God has been faithful to see us through them all.

Love,
Your wife, Barbara J. Collins

Acknowledgments

First and foremost, I would like to thank my Lord and Savior, Jesus Christ, for the wisdom, knowledge, and insight—with much prayer—to write this commentary book. First, I would like to thank my loving wife, Barbara, for her friendship, support, faithfulness to God, and twenty years of marriage. She is my queen! I would like to thank my sister and my brothers for accepting God's calling on my life, always being there for me, and supporting me even when probably sometimes they did not understand what God was doing with me. I want to thank my circle of family, friends, and church family for their prayers and support over the years. I want to thank Ms. Linda Hewlett (senior literary agent), Ms. Mickaila Sands (publication specialist), and all the staff and wonderful people at Christian Faith Publishing Company for putting this book together and publishing this commentary book.

Introduction

James deals with the Christian attitude toward trials and the Word of God. Jewish Christians, upon learning that they were "saved through faith; and that's not of yourselves: it is the gift of God" (Ephesians 2:8) but by the free grace of God in Jesus Christ, relaxed and became idle and restless. James tells them that faith without works is dead and that their faith should result in the very essence of works. The author—in warnings, denunciations, and exhortations—deals with all the practical questions of their social and religious life.

A Synthetic Study of James

Introduction

James, the brother of Jesus Christ and servant of the Lord, was writing to the Jewish Christians who were scattered abroad. He was writing to let them know that they were wrong in their ways. The Jewish Christians thought all they needed was to have faith in God. But James told them that they were wrong in their thinking. He told them that they needed to have faith along with good works.

Central theme

The book of James shows the difference between working faith and nonworking faith.

Analysis

I. By having working faith, we are better able to withstand the various trials and temptations that we face. With nonworking faith, we rely on self-fulfillment (1:2–7).
   A. Working faith
      1. Working faith counts it all as joy when we fall into temptation.
      2. Working faith teaches us to have patience.
      3. Working faith teaches us about being content.
      4. Working faith allows one to realize his/her need in relationship to Jesus Christ.

    B.   Nonworking faith
       1.   Nonworking faith causes us to have doubts.
       2.   Nonworking faith is like having your faith being compared to a wave of sea tossed by the wind.
       3.   Nonworking faith always looks forward to receiving something from the Lord.

II.   Working faith does not mean being poor, while nonworking faith allows one to enjoy his riches (1:8–11).
    A.   Working faith knows his position in Christ.
    B.   Nonworking faith values the pleasures and material things of this world.

III.   Having working faith means not yielding to trials and temptations, while nonworking faith deals with yielding to trials and temptations (1:12–15).
    A.   Working faith
       1.   Working faith is being blessed when enduring temptation.
       2.   Working faith is receiving a crown of life.
       3.   Working faith realizes who our adversary is.
       4.   Working faith is yielding oneself to God in crucial moments.
    B.   Nonworking faith
       1.   Nonworking faith blames God for his own trials and errors.
       2.   Nonworking faith yields to his own desires outside God's provision.
       3.   Nonworking faith which commits sin brings about death later on in life.

IV.   Having working faith, as opposed to having a nonworking faith, and realizing the goodness of God (1:16–18).
    A.   Working faith
       1.   Working faith knows the difference between good and evil and who its authors are.
       2.   Working faith knows that God never changes.
       3.   Working faith acknowledges Christ's death as the means for salvation available to all men.

     B.   Nonworking faith
         1.   Nonworking faith does not believe God is all good.
         2.   Nonworking faith believes that God changes.
         3.   Nonworking faith does not know the significance of Christ's death and their own conversion.

V.   Working faith knows his place in Christ, as opposed to nonworking faith, who does not (1:19–21).
     A.   Working faith
         1.   Working faith is slow to hear.
         2.   Working faith is slow to speak.
         3.   Working faith is slow to show wrath.
     B.   Nonworking faith
         1.   Nonworking faith does not hear.
         2.   Nonworking faith is not slow to speak.
         3.   Nonworking faith is not slow to wrath.

VI.   Having working faith means being a doer of God's Word, while having nonworking faith means being a hearer of God's Word only (1:22–25).
     A.   Working faith
         1.   Working faith hears the Word of God and does something about it.
         2.   Working faith does not forget God's Word.
         3.   Working faith keeps God's laws and statutes and is blessed.
     B.   Nonworking faith
         1.   Nonworking faith is only a hearer of God's Word and does nothing once he hears it.
         2.   Nonworking faith forgets God's Word.
         3.   Nonworking faith does not keep God's laws and statutes and is not going to be blessed.

VII.   Working faith watches what he says with his tongue, while nonworking faith does not (1:26–27).
     A.   Working faith tries to watch what he says with his tongue because of his position in Christ.

B. Nonworking faith does not control his tongue and what he says because his religion is vain.

VIII. Working faith does not show partiality to others, while nonworking faith does (2:1–13).

    A. Working faith
1. Working faith applies the Lord Jesus Christ to his life to respect others.
2. Working faith shows no respect of persons; all are equal.
3. Working faith does not judge.

    B. Nonworking faith
1. Nonworking faith does not apply the love of God in their life properly, so they do not have a respect of persons.
2. Nonworking faith shows respect of persons to the rich and not the poor.
3. Nonworking faith does not show equality and falsely judges others on the bases of what they have and how a person dresses.

IX. Having working faith means putting our faith into action and showing good works, as opposed to nonworking faith, which does not put our faith into action and does not show any works at all (2:14–26).

    A. Working faith
1. Working faith shows good works toward those who are in need.
2. Working faith shows faith by a person's work.
3. Working faith goes hand in hand with works; you cannot have one without the other.
4. Working faith means to be justified before God for doing good to others.

    B. Nonworking faith
1. Nonworking faith does not do good works toward those who are in need.
2. Nonworking faith does not have any good works to show.

        3.   Nonworking faith believes you only need to have faith without works.

        4.   Nonworking faith without works is dead, and a man is not declared righteous before God.

X.   Working faith tries not to offend others with his tongue, while nonworking faith does not care about being offensive to others (3:1–12).

    A. Working faith

        1.   Working faith realizes that we offend all.

        2.   Working faith tries to control his tongue, realizing how much what he says with his tongue can affect others.

XI.   Working faith produces humility, as opposed to nonworking faith, which is proud and boastful (4:1–10).

    A. Working faith

        1.   Working faith asks God for the things that he needs.

        2.   Working faith is given more of God's grace by not being proud.

    B. Nonworking faith

        1.   Nonworking faith feels he does not need God.

        2.   Nonworking faith lusts after his own desires.

        3.   Nonworking faith does not humble himself before God.

        4.   Nonworking faith's wisdom is made of the world and pertains to the wisdom of the world.

XII.   Working faith does not judge his brother, while nonworking faith does (4:11–12).

    A. Working faith

        1.   Working faith does not speak evil of his brother.

        2.   Working faith does not speak evil of the law.

        3.   Working faith knows that God is the only one who can judge a person.

    B. Nonworking faith

        1.   Nonworking faith speaks evil of his brother.

2. Nonworking faith knows what to do, which is right, but does not do anything about it.

XIII. A working-faith lifestyle is centered more on a lifestyle of godliness, as opposed to a nonworking lifestyle, which is focused on being rich (5:1–16).

A. Working faith
1. Working faith labors in the fields of the rich.
2. Working faith cries out loud to God for help when he is being oppressed by the rich.
3. Working faith does not center on the wealth of the poor.
4. Working faith does not rise up against the rich.

B. Nonworking faith
1. Nonworking faith is focused on the material things of this world, such as silver and gold.
2. Nonworking faith cheats others out of their money for their own purposes.
3. Nonworking faith puts down the poor and also kills them.

XIV. Working faith knows to be patient, while nonworking faith leads to doubt (5:7–11).

A. Working faith
1. Working faith always receives results when patient.
2. Working faith waits patiently for Christ's return.
3. Working faith remembers the patience of the prophets.
4. Working faith knows that the end result will be good.

B. Nonworking faith
1. Nonworking faith complains to others when he sees no results.
2. Nonworking faith doubts Christ's return.
3. Nonworking faith does not believe in or take God at His word that what He says, He will do for them.

XV. Working faith knows how to make a commitment and follow through, as opposed to nonworking faith, who makes a commitment and does not carry it out (5:12).
   A. Working faith knows what is involved in making a commitment, which is done before God.
   B. Nonworking faith makes a commitment and could not care less whether God or anybody else objects to him when he does not keep it.

XVI. Working faith knows about prayer and how to go about praying, while nonworking faith does not (5:13–18).
   A. Working faith
      1. Working faith is willing to acknowledge the importance of prayer.
      2. Working faith knows where the power comes from in crucial situations.
      3. Working faith knows that he needs to ask God to forgive him for his sins.
      4. Working faith knows that prayer takes time to be answered. He also knows that he needs to be persistent in his prayers.
   B. Nonworking faith
      1. Nonworking faith is not willing to acknowledge that he needs prayer.
      2. Nonworking faith does not know how to go about getting a prayer through to God.
      3. Nonworking faith does not confess their sins to God.
      4. Nonworking faith sees no need to confess one's sins to another brother.

XVII. Working faith abides in the Word of God, while nonworking faith strays away from the Word of God (5:19–20).
   A. Working faith follows God's Word and obeys His laws.
   B. Nonworking faith does not always follow God's Word or keep His laws.

Conclusion

I believe that the Jewish Christians who were scattered abroad in the book of James (whom James writes to) now have a better understanding of their faith. I believe now they can recognize and see. For a believer, it is not enough to have faith in God alone. One must have working faith in God along with good works, performing the works and acts of the ministry. We as Christian today can obtain value from this book by applying these same principles in our lives today.

The Critical Method

Critical study has two main emphases: historical, or higher criticism, and textual, or lower criticism. *Higher* and *lower* do not refer to ranks but to spheres of origin. Lower criticism deals with the persons, events, and conditions that led to the production of the text (i.e., Does the text reveal a trend, idea, statement, or situation that is incompatible with known history from that time, making it a forgery of the work of a redactor?).

Steps in conducting a critical study

I.   *The authorship of James.* Early scholars believe James is the author because Eusebius says so. We can see the very Jewish said of the Epistle of James, writing style—coming from James, as seen in his epistle.

II.   *The place of writing.* I believe the place of writing of the book of James was in Jerusalem because in Jerusalem, unlike in any other place, we can see the real life of the Jewish people. In the book of James, James addresses Jewish Christians who are scattered abroad. James himself was a leader in the Jerusalem church. He was familiar with the Jewish way of thinking and customs.[1]

III.   *The date of writing.* James was probably written around AD 44. It was the first New Testament book because of how it

---

[1] Justo L. Gonzalez, *The Story of Christianity* (San Francisco: Harper and Row Publishing Company, 1984), 20–21.

pertains to Jesus ascending as the Lord, according to James 1:12. We see that the word *gospel* is not mentioned in the book of James either when dealing with the salvation of men coming to know Jesus Christ. Warnings against being false teachers also points to James being written early.

IV. *The destination of James.* For centuries before the birth of Jesus, the number of Jews living away from Palestine had been increasing. From Old Testament times, there were numerous Jews in Persia and Mesopotamia. In Egypt, they even built a temple in the seventh century BC and another five centuries later. By the time of Jesus, there were sizable Jewish communities in every major city in the Roman Empire. These Jews were scattered all over and whom James refers to in his epistle.

V. *The occasion for the writing.* This is the first Christian response to Hellenism to turn the Jewish Christians who did not understand their faith correctly from the error of their ways, according to James 5:20.[2]

    A. *The Holy Bible (King James Version).* James deals with the materialism in the church. He accuses the church of ignoring God and boasting about themselves. These men had failed to follow the Christian tradition; they had failed to place the whole of their future in the hands of God. We see James giving the application of the teachings of Jesus to the practical problems of the Jewish community.

VI. *The unity of James.* James added to the Old Testament and is cohesive with it. It has the same view of Scripture that was held by the Old Testament writers. The Old Testament scriptures were reliable and responsible not only for spiritual resource but also spiritual growth. We can see the same thing in the book of James when James wrote to the

---

[2] The Holy Bible, King James Version (Iowa Falls, Eyre & Spottiswoode Publishers); Charles F. Pfeiffer and Everett F. Harrison, *The Wycliffe Bible Commentary* (Chicago: Moody Press, 1983).

Jewish Christians scattered abroad. He is writing in regard to them receiving spiritual growth in their lives as mature Christians in Jesus Christ. James is written in Hebrew wisdom like Proverbs. Also, he wrote in the style of Hebrew literature. We know that James recognized the prophets, and that concept from the Old Testament is translated in James.

VII. *The place of James in the New Testament.* James does not contradict itself. It fits the Gospel letters. James is more Catholic in the scope of his epistle writing as opposed to Paul and the other writers. The book of James has but little emphasis on doctrine and theology. Jesus is only mentioned twice.

There is no reference to redemption, the incarnation, or the resurrection. James's main emphasis is on the behavior of the Jewish Christians. James was the first reliable New Testament wisdom. Peter reported to him on his release from prison, and Paul asked for his advice. We know that James was very influential both among the Jews and in the church. He was a pastor in the Judean church. We also see that the Jewish Christians were living in the active and powerful expectation of Christ's imminent return. We see this in 1 and 2 Thessalonians as well.

Conclusion

James, the brother of Jesus Christ, did write the book of James because James was the recognized leader of the Jerusalem church. He had the type of knowledge and insight of one who had great wisdom, as though Jesus might have said the same things Himself to the Jewish Christians if He were there. This book has a number of subjects and teachings on the practical areas of Christian living, which is much needed today. Whether it belongs in the Bible or not or whatever place it should be in the Bible should not be important. That we do have a book such as the book of James in the Bible is important.

The Biographical Method

James, the half brother of Jesus, probably had a rough childhood while growing up in Jerusalem by being the brother of Christ. He probably was always ridiculed for what Jesus said and did. I can picture someone saying to him, "Hey, James! Can your brother make it rain today? He claims to be God!" or "James, does your brother, Jesus, ever get any whippings for doing anything wrong?" And James would replay, "No, He never does because He has never or will ever do anything wrong!"

Another would ask, "James, how come your brother always goes to the temple every day, talking to the religious leader there?"

Then James would probably respond with "Well, He likes to go to the temple. He feels that He knows a lot about certain laws and different things that they do not know about."

I can even see Jesus asking James to go with Him to the temple sometimes and James responding by saying, "I have something else to do right now, and I'm really not that interested in going today. Maybe some other time."

Or how about Mary and Joseph asking James to take the garbage out? James would reply by saying that he always takes the trash out and asks Jesus to take the garbage out sometimes. I can see James's parents telling him to stop reading his books and spending so much time up in his room and that he needs to go outside and play with the other children. I can also see Mary, Joseph, Jesus, and James all sitting together at the dinner table, praying before they would eat their dinner.

Picture this. One day, James and Jesus are walking to school together, and Jesus asks James if he has ever thought about being saved.

"What's being saved?" James asks.

Jesus then tells him, "It is by accepting me as your personal Savior."

James must think that Jesus is crazy!

James, before he goes to bed, probably said his prayers like his mother told him to, like a good little Jewish boy should. I can picture James playing with his friends, them deciding who should be the leader, and them all picking Jesus to be the leader of their game because of how smart they know He is.

The Historical Method

Palestine was the real home of the Jews; and nowhere else but here can we see the real lives of the Jewish people. This was the homeland of the Jews. Palestine, often called the Holy Land, was a tiny country of small dimensions—ten thousand square miles. The entire country could be placed three times in South Carolina, seven times in Missouri, and twenty-six times in Texas. Its importance in world history is out of proportion to its size. It was bordered by the Mediterranean Sea to the west and shared borders with ancient Syria to the north, the Arabian Desert to the east, and a semi-desert country to the south, one occupied through the centuries by many transient peoples.

Canaan is the older name of Palestine. It is derived from the name Hurrian, meaning "belonging to the land of red purple." By the fourteenth century BC, this geographical location came to be called the region in which the Canaanites or Phoenician traders exchanged red-purple dye from murex shells on the Mediterranean coast for other commodities. In Scripture, Canaan is referred to as the Holy Land by God and the people who lived there to be in a covenant relationship with Him.

Palestine has a rainy season and a dry season—two very unvarying periods. The dry season lasts for approximately six months (April to September), during which time, absolutely no rain falls in the country.

In New Testament times, Palestine consisted of Roman Judea, Galilee (our Lord's home, based in the northwest), and Samaria (occupied the central highlands); and Judea extended south to the borders of Idumaea.

Supported by the leaders, Peter and James (the half brother of Jesus), the advice of the influential mother church in Jerusalem clearly favored freedom from the Mosaic Law for Gentile believers but urged Gentiles to avoid practices that would unnecessarily offend Jews like eating meat that had been dedicated to an idol before sale, eating meat from an animal that had been strangled, eating meat that still contained the animal's blood, fornication, or unchastity in general.

The Theological Method

One must first collect the statements under a heading and formulate a doctrinal truth concurrent with the dating of the epistle and then weigh other known theological data bearing the author's intent of writing or the problems addressed in the book.

Bibliology:

1:18	The Word of God is truth.
1:21	God's Word saves our souls.
1:25	Be a doer of the Word.
2:23	Abraham believed God.
4:5	Our flesh is weak.
4:11	Judge not.
5:11	Have the patience of Job.
5:12	Do not make a commitment to God if you cannot keep it.

General truth or doctrinal statement: The Old Testament Scriptures are reliable and responsible not for spiritual resource but for spiritual growth. It is the same view of Scripture that was held by the Old Testament writers.

Theology proper:

1:33	God is not the author of evil.
1:17	God never changes.
1:18	God's will.
2:19	The oneness of God.

General truth or doctrinal statement: I believe in one unchanging God.

Angelology—general truth or doctrinal statement: James does not make mention of angels in his epistle.

Anthropology:

1:7	Man is proud.
1:8	Man changes.
1:13	God does not tempt man.
2:3	Man shows partiality.
2:18	Man relies on his own good works once saved.
3:8	Man cannot tame his tongue.
3:9	Man was created in God's own image.
5:3	Man stores up earthly riches.
5:16	A righteous man's prayers are answered by God

General truth or doctrinal statement: Outside God, man is lost. Man needs someone to direct his ways and steps. He needs a loving, kind, and triune God.

Hamartiology:

1:13–16	God cannot be tempted by evil.
1:21	The things of the world are sinful.
2:9	Showing partiality is committing a sin.
2:10–11	Not keeping the faith and God's Word is a sin.
4:4	Being friends with the world is a sin.
4:17	We commit a sin when we know to do what is right but not do it.
5:19–20	When one leads a fallen brother back from his evil ways, his sin is no longer held against him.

General truth or doctrinal statement: The thing that is not of God's nature is sin because God is not the author of evil. Satan is the ruler of this world and the author of evil. God sent His Son, Jesus Christ, to die for the sins of the world.

Soteriology:

1:5–6	We are to pray and ask God for wisdom.
2:26	The body is dead without the spirit.
5:14–15	The elders of the church are to pray for the sick.

General truth or doctrinal statement: God is personally involved and active in the life of the believer. The prayer of faith helps those who need wisdom, and who are sick.

Ecclesiology:

2:1	It is inconsistent to hold to the Christian faith and at the same time show partiality.
2:6–8	Rich man's motives in the church.
4:1	Moral problems in the church.

General truth or doctrinal statement: The church should not be corrupt or partial in their ways but pleasing to the Lord in every way in spite of the conditions and problems that they may have by applying the teachings of Jesus Christ to their situations.

Eschatology:

1:1	The Christian Church is called New Israel.
5:7–11	Exhortating the church in view of Christ's returning.

General truth or doctrinal statement: We as Christians need to suffer and endure with a patient attitude. The church needs to hold together in spite of the intense pressures that they may be faced with while anticipating the expedient return of our Lord.

Christology:

1:1	A servant of God and Jesus Christ.
1:12	The Lord promises the faithful man the crown of life.
4:15	Say, "If the Lord wills it" in our decision-making.
5:4	The Lord of Sabath is sovereign.
5:7–8	The Lord's Second Coming.

5:11	The Lord has some end or blessing for us in our trials and temptations.
5:16	The Lord heals the sick and forgives sins.
5:17	The Lord answers prayer.

General truth or doctrinal statement: The Lord is the only one who can forgive us for our sins. He is the only one that we can go to, to be saved. The Lord Jesus Christ is coming back again for His people soon. We as servants of Jesus Christ will be with Him in heaven one day to spend all of eternity. The Lord directs all our ways and steps.

Pneumatology:

2:26	Having the body and the spirit.
4:5	God's spirit dwells in us.

General truth or doctrinal statement: The Holy Spirit lives in the life of the believer. We as Christians have life because the Holy Spirit lives in us. If a Christian does not have God's spirit dwelling in him, there is no life. Having life is the result of having both the body and the spirit in the life of the believer. But when you do not have the two or they become separate, death results.

The Rhetorical Method

The rhetorical method indicates how the use of syntax and figures of speech are employed to convey doctrinal and other types of teaching employed by the author in the book.

A simile is an expressed comparison between two objects that are materially unrelated to each other, usually denoted by *like* or *as*.

1:6	But let him ask in faith, nothing wavering for he that wavereth is like a wave of the sea driven with the wind and tossed.	James compares a man doubtful in faith to the wave of the sea, driven to and fro by the wind.
1:10	But the rich, in that he is made low: because as the flower of the grass he shall pass away.	James is saying that riches are temporary, like a flower.
1:23	For if any be a hearer of the word, and not a doer, he is like unto a man beholding his natural face in a glass.	James compares being a doer of God's Word to a man who looks at himself in a mirror and forgets what he looks like.
2:8	If ye fulfill the royal law according to the scripture, thou shall love thy neighbor as thyself, ye do well.	James is comparing us loving our fellow man to how we love ourselves.

2:26	For as the body without the Spirit is dead, so faith without works is dead.	James is comparing our bodies when we have the Spirit living in us and when we have faith and not works. He says that to have one without the other is to be spiritually dead.

A metaphor is a comparison between two objects suggested by the substitution of the name of one for the name of the other.

1:18	Of his own will begat he us with the word of truth, that we should be a kind of first fruits of his creatures.	The new life in Christ because of our new birth or regeneration.
1:25	But whoso looketh into the perfect law of liberty, and continueth therein, he being not a forgetful hearer, but a doer of the work, this man shall be a blessing in his deed.	James is talking about the teachings of Christ.
3:5	Even so the tongue is a little member, and boasteth great things. Behold, how great a matter a little fire kindeleth.	James is comparing our tongue to a fire.
4:4	Ye adulterers and adulteresses, know ye not that the friendship of the world is emnity with God? Whosoever therefore will be a friend of the world is the enemy of God.	James is talking about being involved in the things not of God.

4:14	Whereas ye know not what shall be on the morrow. For what is your life? It is even a vapor, that appeareth for a little time, and then vanisheth away.	James is comparing our life to vapor; one minute we can be here, and the next minute we can be gone.

An allegory is an extended simile or metaphor by which the details of a story are made to convey a meaning different from the literal meaning of the events recorded.

1:9–11	Let the brother of low degree rejoice in that he is exalted. But the rich, in that he is made, low because as the flower of the grass he shall pass away. For the sun is no sooner risen with a burning heart but it withereth the grass, and the flower thereof falleth, and the grace of the fashion of it perisheth, so also shall the rich man fade away in his ways.	James talks about how a flower dies, and this is in reference to what will happen to a rich man in regard to how he treats the poor.
2:21–26	Was not Abraham our father justified by works, when he had offered Isaac his son upon the altar? Seest thou how faith wrought with his works, and by his works was faith made perfect? And the scripture was fulfilled which saith, Abraham believed God, and it was imputed unto him for righteousness, and he was called the	Faith without some type of action is not having a faith at all. Abraham showed action by offering up his son Isaac to God. Rahab, the harlot, had received the messengers and sent them out another way. These people both put their faith into practice.

	friend of God. Ye see then how that by works a man is justified, and not by faith only. Likewise also was not Rahab the harlot justified by works, when she had received the messengers, and had sent then out another way? For as the body without the spirit is dead, so faith without works is dead also.	
3:2–8	For in many things we offend all. If any man offend not in word, the same is a perfect man, and able also to bridle the whole body. Behold, we put bits in the horses' mouths, that they may obey us; and we turn about their whole body. Behold also the ships which though they be great, and are driven of fierce winds, yet are they turned about with a very small helm, whithersoever the governor listeth. Even so the tongue, is a little member, and boasteth great things. Behold, how great a matter a little fire kindeleth! And the tongue is a little member, and boasteth great things. Behold, how great a matter a little fire kindeleth! And the tongue is a fire, a world of iniquity, so is the tongue among our members, that it defileth the whole body, and setteth on	Man cannot tame his tongue. James compares the tongue to how a horse turns his whole body when you put a bit in his mouth. He compares the tongue to a ship, how a wind can turn a ship to and fro. James gives examples to show us how harmful our tongues can be with just the mere words we say.

	fire the course of nature, and it is set on fire of hell. For every kind of beasts, and of birds, and of serpents, and of things in the sea is tamed, and hath been tamed of mankind. But the tongue can no man tame; it is an unruly evil, full of deadly poison.	
5:7–8	Be patient therefore, brethren, unto the coming of the Lord. Behold, the husbandman waiteth for the precious fruit of the earth, and hath long patience for it, until he receive the early and latter rain. Be ye also patient; stablish your hearts, for the coming of the Lord draweth nigh.	James talks about how the husbandman waits for the fruit of the earth to appear, in retrospect to a Christian who awaits Jesus Christ's Second Coming.

A metonymy is the use of a word for another that it suggests, such as the effect for the cause or the causes for the effect.

1:3	Testing and faith.
1:13	Satan is the author of evil.
1:18	Faith and works.
4:3	Ask not and receive not.
4:5	God's spirit dwells in us, and He should be our only act of worship.
4:7	Trust God, and Satan will flee.
4:11	Judge and become not a doer of the law.
5:11	Job had patience, and God is sovereign.
5:17	Pray, and God will bless.
5:20	Salvation and repentance.

A synecdoche is the use of a part to represent the whole or the use of the whole to represent the part.

1:2	To be happy when trials come.
1:5	If you need wisdom, then ask God for it.
1:12	Man is blessed when he endured trials.
1:26	If a man cannot control his tongue, then his religion is worthless.
2:2–3	Do not show any partiality between those who are rich and those who are poor.
2:5	God has chosen the poor to be the heirs of the kingdom.
2:17	Faith without works is dead.
3:9	The damage that our tongues can do.
4:11	For us not to judge our brothers.
5:7–8	That believers should look forward to Christ's Second Coming.
5:11	God is sovereign.
5:17	To always pray, continually.
5:20	To restore a brother who has fallen into sin.

A hyperbole is an exaggeration for the sake of emphasis.

2:2–3	Rich man in good apparel, a poor man in vile raiment, and a rich man in gay clothing.
2:19	"Do thy believest that there is one God? The demons also believe and tremble."
3:6	"Tongue setteth on fire the course of nature."
3:8	"Tongue…an unruly evil full of deadly poison."
4:14	Our life, like a vapor, appears for a while, then vanishes away.
5:12	Above all things, do not make a commitment you cannot keep to God.

Irony is when a statement is made contrary to an existing fact to emphasize its actuality.

1:9	A double-minded man is unstable in all of his ways.
1:10	The rich man made low.
1:23	To be a hearer of the word and not just a doer.
1:26	If any man is religious and cannot bridle his tongue, his religion is in vain.
2:10	When one keeps the whole law yet breaks one, one is guilty of them all.
2:11	Committing adultery and killing someone is being a transgressor of the law.
4:2	You have not because you ask not.
4:4	Being a friend of the world means being an enemy of God.

Litotes are the affirmation of a fact by denying its opposite.

1:13	God is not the author of evil; therefore, God does not tempt any to do evil.
2:19	There is only one God who has great power.

A meiosis is an understatement of truth for the sake of emphasis, the opposite of hyperbole.

5:17–18	Elias was a man like us who was also subject to sin, like we are today. He prayed that it might not rain, and it did not rain for three years. He was a man of prayer.

A euphemism is the substitution of a mild expression for a term that might be violent or coarse, although the significance of the literal fact is attached to it.

1:15	The rich man fades away, lust leads to sin, and sin leads to death.
4:8	Draw nigh to God, and He will draw nigh to you!
4:14–15	We do not know what will happen to tomorrow, so we should say, "If the Lord wills."
5:12	"But above all things, my brethren, swear not."

A rhetorical question is a question that calls for no direct answer to attract the attention of the hearer.

2:14	"What doth it profit, my brethren, though a man say he hath faith, and have not works? Can faith save him?"
2:16	"And one of you say unto them, depart in peace, be ye warmed and filled; not withstanding ye give them not those things which are needful to the body, what doth it profit?"
2:20	"But wilt thou know, O vain man, that faith without works is dead?"
2:21	"Was not Abraham our father justified by works, when he had offered Isaac his son upon the altar?"
3:11	"Doth a fountain send forth at the same place sweet water and bitter?"
3:12	"Can the fig tree, my brethren, bear dive berries? either a vine, figs? So can no fountain both yield salt water and fresh."

| 4:1 | "From whence come wars and fightings among you? Come they not hence, even of your lusts that war in your members?" |
| 4:14 | "Whereas ye know not what shall be on the morrow. For what is your life? It is even a vapour, that appeareth for a little time, and then vanisheth away." |

The Topical Method

Throughout each book of the Bible runs a web of topical structure forming the main ideas that the author wants to communicate. Topical themes can be the main subject of the book and ancillary. Each topic is important because God does not waste words. He wants us to know Him.

Trials

Trials are important to a believer. Trials in a believer's life are the testing of a believer's faith. The trials or testing help us as Christians be what God would have us be as we go through them. They help us trust God more. They help us build character and have a more committed and devoted life to God. Trials come because Jesus Christ suffered also, and God's Word tells us that as He suffered, we as Christians are going to suffer also. James tells us to count it all as joy when we fall into divers temptations (count it as a blessing). He goes on to say that the trying of a believer's faith "worketh patience." It helps us be a little more patient with God when we do not see Him working in our lives, especially when the trials come. James goes further to say that if we do not understand why these trials come, we need to ask God for wisdom to help us understand the reason we are suffering.

Temptation

We are all susceptible to temptation. There is none righteous in God's sight. Jesus Christ was the only one that was perfect. Satan tried Jesus, and He did not give in! We as Christians must not give in to the temptations when they come because the end result can have a tremendous effect in the life of a believer. James tells us that temptation leads to sin and that sin leads to death. He also tells us that if we abstain from temptation, we will receive a crown of life at the end. God will bless us for it when we get to heaven. James reminds us as Christians that God does not tempt us. Some Christians believe that God is tempting them to commit sin. But James tells us that God is not the author of evil and that God does not tempt man to do evil.

Partiality

God shows no respect of person. He sent His only Son Jesus Christ to die for all mankind. God has no respect of persons. We all are equal and precious in God's sight. God cares about the poor as well as the rich. He just blesses some more than others, that's all! But we should not look down on those because we have more than they do, nor should we treat them differently because James says that is sin. Showing respect to others because of one's financial status is wrong.

James goes on to say that God has chosen the poor of this world to be rich in faith and the heirs of the kingdom of God, which he has promised to them that love Him. James goes on to say that a rich man has riches but will one day fade away. God wants us to build our riches in heaven rather than on earth because one day, just like the rich man, they will pass away. But if we give our tithes and our offerings to God, we will be blessed for it in heaven because we know that what we do for Christ will last for all eternity.

God, in His Word, also said that it will be hard for a rich man to enter the kingdom of heaven. We need to know that God shows no respect of persons, so why do we, especially if we claim to be Christlike?

Faith and works

We as Christians need to have faith along with works. It is not enough to just have faith and not have works to go along with our faith. James says that faith without works is dead. We need to put our faith into action. We need to produce some fruit (figuratively) from our lives. God wants us to help others come into the saving knowledge of Jesus Christ. He wants us to minister to our brothers and sisters who are in need and do not have the knowledge of the Word as well with our money and time. God wants us to meet their physical needs as well as their spiritual needs. James says, "Show me thy faith without thy works, and I will show thee my faith by my works" (James 1:18). I would seriously doubt whether a person is a Christian or not if he does not have any fruit in his life. We know great men of the Bible that showed and produced some type of fruit in their lives in serving God. They put their faith into action rather than sitting back and doing nothing. We ought to put our faith into action and go out and help somebody else, whether meeting a physical need (whatever that may be) or spiritual need. We need to stop talking so much about our faith and to put it into practice.

Tongue

What we say with our tongues can be more harmful then we think as a Christian. When you say something bad with your tongue, you cannot take it back and fix what you have said. The damage has already been done, and James 3:5 said that "the tongue is a little member, and boasteth great things. Behold, how great a matter a little fire kindeleth!" The tongue and what we say with our tongue can ruin and destroy a person's reputation, and we cannot control what we say with our tongue without Jesus Christ living in our hearts. James 3:8 says, "No man can control the tongue; it is an unruly evil, full of deadly poison." Without a personal relationship with Jesus Christ, our tongue will continue to rule us. God will be able, then, once we accept Jesus Christ as our Savior, to help us control our thought patterns and what we say. We no longer will be thinking or saying the things the way the world says and thinks of certain things. We become a new creature in Christ, and the old nature passes away.

James 3:6 says, "The tongue is like a fire, and that it defileth the whole body." Without Christ in our lives, we are lost because He is the one who takes control over our lives and bodies once we commit our lives to Him. Our tongues become more in tune with God's thought patterns, and we no longer let our tongues rule over us.

God's will

We need to follow God's laws along with the laws of our own government. But we should dwell more on what God's will is. He should be our main focus. Our eyes should remain focused on Him alone. Everything we do and say should be pleasing to Him. Our desire should be about our Father's business.

Jesus Christ was our perfect example to follow while He was here on earth. He did not get caught up in the things of the world. He was committed to His Father the way we should be committed to God. Also, James 4:8 says, "We need to draw nigh to God, and he will draw nigh to you." If we do God's will or keep our minds on Him, we will not say anything bad about others and will not find fault in our brothers. We would just pray for them and love them in spite of their faults.

We should not let anyone keep us from doing God's will. We should love God and be willing to do whatever and go wherever God calls us to do and go, with our mind and attitude focused on Him, doing only the things that are according to His will for our lives.

Prayer

Prayer should be done continuously in the life of a believer. Scripture teaches us that we are to always pray daily. Prayer is where the power comes from in the life of a believer. James 5:16 says, "The effectual fervent prayer of a righteous man availeth much." A lot of great preachers would not have been great preachers without praying for themselves and having others pray for them too. Prayer is important. Prayer can change things. James 5:15 says, "The prayer of faith shall save the sick."

We find in the Scriptures that Jesus Christ took time to pray (Mark 14:35–36). He also taught His disciples the Lord's prayer (Matthew 6:9–13). And His disciples prayed too. Are we better than Jesus Christ and His disciples? We need to pray just like they prayed. When we pray, we need to ask God to forgive us for our sins. James says that we need to confess our faults to one another and pray for one another so that we may be healed.

Scripture teaches us that God will not hear our prayers if we have any sin in our hearts when we pray (Isaiah 59:2) We need patience when we do not receive an answer from God. Scripture teaches us to pray without ceasing. Do not give up when you don't receive an answer right away. Keep on praying, and your answer will come in due time. In the Black churches, we say, "God might not come when you want Him to come. But He's always right on time."

The Analytical Method

I. Salutation (1:1)

II. Trials (1:2–18)
    A. The purpose of trials (1:12)
    B. How to endure trials (1:13–16)
    C. Comfort in our Trials (1:17–18)

III. Temptation (1:19–21)
    A. Do not become angry (1:19–20)
    B. Putting away the old nature (1:21)

IV. Yielding to God's Word (1:22–27)
    A. Being a doer of God's Word (1:22–25)
    B. Applying God's Word to our lives (1:26–27)

V. Partiality (2:1–13)
    A. Showing respect of persons (2:1–4)
    B. The poor are blessed (2:5–7)
    C. Breaking God's commandment (2:8–11)
    D. Conscious of breaking God's laws (2:12–13)

VI. Faith and works (2:14–26)
    A. Having an inactive faith without works (2:14–17)
    B. Having an active faith with works (2:18–26)

VII. Tongue (3:1–18)
    A. Bridle the tongue (3:1–5a)
    B. Tongue like a fire (3:5b–12)

VIII. Wisdom (3:13–18)
    A. Conversation (3:13–14)
    B. Wisdom from above (3:15–18)

IX.   The sinful acts of man (4:1–10)
    A.   Being of the world (4:1–5)
    B.   Humility (4:6–10)
X.   Judging others (4:11–12)
XI.   God's will (4:13–17)
    A.   Making our own plans (4:13–15)
    B.   Boasting (4:16–17)
XII.   The ways of the rich man (5:1–6)
XIII.   Having patience (5:7–11)
    A.   Anticipating Christ's second coming (5:8)
    B.   Do not envy those who are prosperous (5:9)
    C.   Looking at the prophets before us (5:10–11)
XIV.   Do not make a commitment to God if you cannot keep it (5:12)
XV.   Prayer (5:13–18)
    A.   Pray for the sick (5:13)
    B.   Call the elders of the church to pray (5:14)
    C.   Pray while believing your request will be answered (5:15)
    D.   Confess your sins and pray for one another (5:16)
    E.   Be persistent in your prayers (5:17–18)
XVI.   Backslider (5:19–20)
    A.   Carnal Christian being restored (5:19)
    B.   Safe from God's wrath (5:20)

The Comparative Method

James's belief in the realm of spiritual growth is the same as the view of the Scripture that was held by the Old Testament writers. The Old Testament writers viewed the Scriptures as being reliable and responsible not only for spiritual resource but also spiritual growth. James held this view in writing his pastoral letter to the Jews who were scattered abroad to teach them to have a more active spiritual life and bear fruit. James also can be compared to some New Testament writers too because James lays out some specific principles and points out that in a Christian life, we need to follow and obey. We can see some of these same kinds of principles and standards to follow in the New Testament by our New Testament writers.

New Testament	Old Testament
James 1:1	Genesis 49:28
James 1:5	Proverbs 2:6
James 1:5	1 Chronicles 22:12
James 1:13	Deuteronomy 6:16
James 1:13	Job 34:12
James 2:1	2 Chronicles 19:7
James 2:5	1 Samuel 2:8
James 2:8	Leviticus 19:18
James 2:11	Deuteronomy 5:18
James 2:11	Exodus 20:13–14
James 2:16	Job 22:7

James 2:21	Genesis 22:12
James 2:23	Genesis 15:6
James 3:2	Psalm 39:1
James 3:3	Psalm 32:9
James 3:8	Psalm 52:2–4
James 4:6	Proverbs 20:7
James 4:10	2 Chronicles 34:27
James 4:11	Leviticus 20:15
James 4:15	Judges 18:5
James 5:12	Deuteronomy 23:21
James 5:12	Numbers 30:2
James 5:15	Exodus 40:15
James 5:16	Proverbs 15:29
James 5:20	Isaiah 63:17

New Testament	New Testament
James 1:1	Romans 1:1
James 1:2	Matthew 5:11–12
James 1:2	2 Corinthians 1:4–5
James 1:2	2 Corinthians 6:10
James 1:22	Romans 2:13
James 1:23–24	1 Corinthians 2:14
James 2:8	Matthew 22:39
James 2:9	Romans 2:11
James 2:14	Ephesians 2:8–9
James 2:17	Galatians 3:12
James 2:21	Hebrews 11:17
James 2:23	Romans 4:1–22
James 2:23	Galatians 3:6
James 3:5–6	Ephesians 4:29
James 4:2–3	Philippians 4:6

James 4:4	Colossians 3:1
James 4:10	Philippians 2:3–9
James 4:11	Romans 2:1
James 4:13	Matthew 6:25
James 4:15	Acts 21:14
James 5:15	Ephesians 1:5
James 5:10	Acts 15:15
James 5:11	2 Timothy 2:12
James 5:13	Colossians 3:16
James 5:16	1 Thessalonians 5:17

The Devotional Method

All our previous study methods have given us a well-rounded knowledge of James, but a mere knowledge of these facts misses the real purpose for which we study—that we integrate and apply the truths of God's Word to our lives so that we may grow in our personal relationship with Jesus Christ and then in turn, edify other believers and evangelize the unsaved.

Personally, looking back at the book of James, I learned to be happy when I am faced with trials and temptations. First, I realize that the trials come to help me strive toward perfection. God sometimes allows us to go through things for His glory so that we can become more like Him (Leviticus 19:2). God wants us to be fit for the kingdom. Our trials are there to help us to be more of what God desires us to be, and that is to be conformed to the image of His Son, Jesus Christ. Second, Jesus Christ dealt with temptation, and are we any better than He? Besides that, God's Word says that we are going to suffer because of Christ. Are we better than Jesus Christ? So when James says to be happy, I can be encouraged to know that I am going through the same things that Christ went through while He was here on earth. I am encouraged because just as Jesus was victorious over temptation, we can be too. Paul also said that we do still have a sinful nature in us but that we can be victorious by giving our bodies and minds fully over to the Lord.

I learned that God is not the author of evil. I knew He was not, but fully seeing it in Scripture helps you know that God is not behind all the evil in this world. God cannot tempt man to do evil. That it is not in His nature. This is a blessing. Applying this theological statement to my life lets me know that all the bad things that happen to me are not because of God. My perspective of how God works is a little bit clearer.

I learned that faith without works is dead, as James said. We as Christians need to make disciples and produce fruit, figuratively speaking. It is not enough for a Christian to just have faith alone. The believer must act on that faith by going about and doing the ministry. We need to spread the good news whenever we have a chance to. If I am not producing fruit or making disciples, then I must examine my Christian life to see if I have truly been born again.

I learned to control what I may say and how much I can do to people by what I say. The things I say with my tongue cannot be taken back. James says that the tongue is so bad that it is like a fire. You cannot tame it. My tongue can really destroy a person by what I say with it. I need to be careful in what I say to people. I believe that through what I say and how I say things to people, I can build them up or tear them down.

I need to be in constant prayer every day. I need to say, "Lord, help me control my tongue, what I say to people." I believe I need to let God control my thinking pattern. Application requires that I pray much and yield my body to the Lord.

To me prayer is the key to the Christian life. I believe that when a Christian prays daily, there is much power, and less praying results in less power. We know that Jesus Christ prayed, and He is our example. If we want to be more like Him, then we should pray. He told us to pray constantly and without ceasing. Besides that, I believe prayer is where the power comes from. Application for me requires that I pray daily so I will not be subjected to Satan. Prayer does not always have to be long. But we need to always have a prayer in our hearts. If we are going to defeat Satan, we must be about prayer. James 5:16 says that "the effectual fervent prayer of a righteous man availeth much." Jesus says that some things can only be done by prayer and fasting. In our prayers, we need to be patient too, especially when we do not get an answer right away. Someone once said that God's time is not our time. James tells us to be patient as well.

We need to restore a brother once he has fallen into sin. We are all saved by grace, and we all have sinned. We all have skeletons in our closets. And as Scripture says, "Let him who is without sin cast the first stone" (John 8:7). In other words, don't condemn your brother.

We have a loving Father who is willing to forgive us of our sins, so why should we not forgive a brother when he sins? God wants all of us to be saved and have fellowship with Him. Application for me requires that I not look down on my Christian brothers and sisters once they have fallen into sin because that can happen to me but restore them, just like the story of the prodigal son—how a loving father took his son back when he left home to go into the evil world. God is the same way with us if we repent.

Bibliography

Adamson, James B. *The Epistle of James.* Grand Rapids: William B. Eerdmans Publishing Company, 1976.

Davids, Peter H. *The Epistle of James: A Commentary on the Greek Text.* Grand Rapids: William B. Eerdmans Publishing Company, 1982.

Gonzalez, Justo L. *The Story of Christianity.* Vol. 1. San Francisco: Harper Row Publishers, 1984.

Hester, H. I. *The Heart of the New Testament.* Liberty, Missouri: The Quality Press Inc., 1963.

Pfeiffer, Charles F., and Everett F. Harrison. *The Wycliffe Bible Commentary.* Chicago: Moody Press, 1983.

Robertson, Archibald Thomas. *Studies in the Epistle of James.* Nashville: Broadman Press, 1915.

The Holy Bible: King James Version. Iowa Falls, Iowa: World Bible Publishers Inc.

What is your prayer request today? Write down your prayer of faith.

About the Author

Reverend Loyce C. Collins was raised on the west side of Chicago, Illinois, by a loving mother and father who had seven children—six boys and one girl. He received Jesus Christ as his personal Savior at an early age while attending a Billy Graham youth conference with his church (Austin Wesleyan Methodist Church) youth group in Chicago, Illinois. Collins accepted his call to the ministry at nineteen years old.

He attended Wilbur Wright Junior College in Chicago, Illinois, where Collins received his certificate in general studies. In 1988, he attended Southwestern Conservative Baptist Bible College, now called Arizona Christian University, located in Phoenix, Arizona. This is where he received his bachelor of science degree in general Bible from Arizona Christian University in 1992.

Collins is a retired chaplain with the Arizona Department of Corrections. He lives in Laveen, Arizona, with his wife, Barbara. Also, Collins currently attends Pilgrim Rest Baptist Church under the leadership of Rev. Dr. Terry E. Mackey. Collins enjoys spending time with family and friends.